`GW00578687`

Trinity Colle

1

By Peter Fox

A great library is the heart of every great university, and the Library of Trinity College has for centuries played a major role in attracting both visitors and scholars to the College.

The 'College of the Holy and Undivided Trinity near Dublin' was founded in 1592 by Queen Elizabeth I. Within ten years of this date there is already evidence that the College possessed a collection of books and manuscripts – a library in fact. One of the oldest existing documents relating to the history of the College, known as the *Particular Book of Trinity College*, contains a list of thirty books and ten manuscripts which belonged to the Library on 24 February 1600/1 **(1)**.

This meagre collection was obviously felt to be inadequate for a growing university, and so, in the same year, two of the College's Fellows, Luke Challoner and James Ussher (the future Archbishop of Armagh), were sent off to England to buy books to augment the Library. They bought extensively, and as a result of their purchases the Library grew rapidly. Some of the receipts for these books still exist, showing the date of purchase, the name of the bookseller and a list of the titles bought. Challoner and Ussher did most of their buying in London, where no doubt they met Sir Thomas Bodley who was engaged on a similar errand for his new library in Oxford, but they also travelled to Oxford and Cambridge in

search of items for purchase. It is far from clear where the money for this book-buying expedition came from. According to an old legend, the victorious English soldiers who defeated the Irish and Spaniards at the Battle of Kinsale in 1602 donated £1,800 for the purchase of books for Trinity College Library. A more likely – if mundane – explanation is that private donations and government grants, perhaps partly based on back-pay due to the soldiers, were the source of the finance.

Of the Elizabethan College buildings nothing now exists, although the coat of arms of Queen Elizabeth I, which is now on display in the Long Room, is believed to have come from the original College Chapel **(2)**. At this time the College consisted of two-storeyed brick buildings surrounding a small square courtyard, and the Library occupied the upper storey of the south wing, over the students' living quarters. There is an inventory of College possessions made

1 (*inside front cover*). The first Library catalogue (1600/1) in the *Particular Book of Trinity College*.

2 (*right*). Coat of arms of Queen Elizabeth I.

feist albas ad larga psidia mi soz.
Theam macq i signis xpi martyris
que ex argento ʒ auro uetusto instruit
ope copiosa paupibz dispsit laricate.
Exemplum hoc facto beati seatuis
leuite laureni qui thesauros eccie
pia uoluit libalitate egenis distribue
re ne posset auara manus censum que
sibi pepit ʒ eo aduaret inuenire. Expo
liauit itacq beatum martirem alba
nu illa sui uasis temporali tunica. ut
elegantiore reparata idem uestiri me
ret eciam. Cou regi nondua nō pncipi
aliquod uir egregius optulit inde

minus factum ʒ totu satis usibz eribu
it egenoz. Displit ut ait dauid. dedit
paupibz iustitia ei manet i eteruum.
Et eum remuniator ueuit i maies
tate sua. cornu ei exaltabit ī glia
Hormam uniuisis eo i tempore ec
lesis epstit. ut imei uitas secoz opus
fabricaret ʒ speciali. ʒ hunc mo
rem imitaret noua semp genisso
futuroz. Dedit itacq opam plarius
minister xpi fabricale hoc sit p teu
bus coparatu. qualem huicemodi
nec autea uidimus. nec quemqua ac
ceptura in anglorum regno uiscuru

in 1608, and among the items belonging to the Library it lists. 'three tables uppon frames, a table of benefactors, 12 great mapps besides many of the lesser, a sceliton with taffety hangings, a table with two globes . . .'.

After Challoner's and Ussher's purchases at the beginning of the century, the Library seems to have grown slowly and to have had no significant accessions until 1661, when it came into the possession of more than 10,000 books and manuscripts from Archbishop Ussher's personal collection (3). Contained in this collection were many important items, including such manuscripts as the *Book of St Albans* (4) and the *Ricemarch Psalter* (5). Ussher had been in England in 1640 and had been forced to remain there on the outbreak of the war in Ireland in the following year. At his death in 1656 his books were housed in Lincoln's Inn in London. He had intended to leave them to Trinity College, so that, after his death, they would find their place in its Library alongside those books which he had bought for the Library fifty years earlier. However, as a result of the war, his income from the archdiocese of Armagh had ceased. He had, therefore, nothing to bequeath to his daughter except his books, to do with as she pleased.

Her husband, Sir Timothy Tyrrell, immediately put the collection up for sale. Among the prospective purchasers were the King of Denmark, Cardinal Mazarin, Sion College in London and the University of Oxford, but Oliver Cromwell forbade Tyrrell to sell the books without his permission. Cromwell and his brother Henry, his lord-deputy in Ireland, had plans to establish a second college in the University of Dublin (Cromwell College), and accordingly decided that Ussher's books

3. Bust of James Ussher in the Long Room.

4. *Book of St Albans* (MS 177) – building St Albans abbey church.

should be bought and sent to Ireland to form the nucleus of a library for this new college. The Restoration of Charles II in 1660 caused this scheme for the creation of a new college to be abandoned, and in 1661 the Irish House of Commons voted to transfer Ussher's library to Trinity College, which remains today the sole college in the University of Dublin.

At about this time the Library received two of its greatest treasures, the *Book of Kells* and the *Book of Durrow*, both of them gifts from Henry Jones, Bishop of Meath, who had earlier been Vice-Chancellor of the University.

In the latter part of the seventeenth century the Library was allowed to fall into a state of disorder, to such an extent that one correspondent, in 1705, could say that 'it is quite neglected and in no order, and on that account is become perfectly useless'. During the rebuilding of the Dining Hall, for example, the Library was used for

5. *Ricemarch Psalter* (MS 50) – Quid gloriaris.

6. George Berkeley, Bishop of Cloyne, College Librarian, 1709.

Commons (dinner) and many of the books were simply moved elsewhere to create the necessary space for the tables. In 1689 it narrowly escaped destruction by fire, when the College was occupied by James II's troops during his Irish campaign. The soldiers caused much damage to the other College buildings, but the Reverend Michael Moore, whom James had appointed Provost in 1689, prevented them from setting fire to the Library.

In 1709 the Library's fortunes began to improve again with the appointment of George Berkeley, the philosopher, as Librarian **(6)**. Berkeley complained about the inadequacy of the Library building, which was still the original one of Elizabeth I's day. He persuaded the College to appeal through the Irish House of Commons to Queen Anne for funds to build a new library. A Parliamentary grant of £5,000 was made and on 12 May 1712 the foundation stone of the new library was laid in the presence of the Provost and Fellows. In 1732, after two further sums of £5,000 had been granted, the building was completed.

This great Library, which formed a part of the eighteenth-century rebuilding of the College, was designed by

A Prospect of the Library of Trinity College DUBLIN. Vûe de la Bibliotèque du Collège de la Trinité à DUBLEN.

Thomas Burgh, Chief Engineer and Surveyor-General of Her Majesty's Fortifications in Ireland. Burgh took as a model Sir Christopher Wren's library at Trinity College, Cambridge, which had been completed in 1699, but set out to surpass it in size and grandeur. A significant feature of both libraries was the placing of the books on an upper floor above an open colonnade, a precaution designed to protect them from damp, for in Burgh's day the Liffey, like the Cam at the other Trinity, came up to the walls of the College. The modern visitor must imagine a more elegant exterior than the one now visible, with the main part of the ground floor consisting of an open arcade divided longitudinally by a central wall and a roof which scarcely rose above the level of the stone balustrade **(7)**.

The Long Room on the first floor truly deserves its name, being 64 metres (209 feet) in length and 12 metres (40 feet) wide. Like the outside of the building, the interior has been considerably altered – though more successfully than the exterior – since 1732. It originally had a flat plaster ceiling, above the level of the gallery **(8)**. In each of the bays there were double benches, which have since been replaced with low

7. The Library in the eighteenth century, showing the open arcades on the ground floor.

bookcases. These benches allowed the reader to sit between the cases and rest his book on a shelf projecting from the case in front of him **(back cover)**. From the beginning the Long Room had a gallery, though it is difficult to imagine why it was felt to be necessary in 1732 as the collections at the time would have filled only a fraction of the shelf space in the room and accessions were relatively few. Two magnificent oak staircases at the west end gave access to the gallery **(9)**. Such was the fear of fire that the building had no provision for heat or light.

On 20 November 1733 the Librarian, Edward Hudson, received £60 for removing the books from the old library and placing them in the Long Room, and during the next four years many of the books, which had suffered considerable neglect in their former accommodation, were rebound. The great donations – Ussher's library, that of William Palliser, Archbishop of Cashel, bequeathed in 1726, and that of Claudius Gilbert, Vice-Provost and Professor of Divinity – were kept together when they were placed in the Long

8. The Long Room in the eighteenth century. Watercolour by James Malton.

Room and the names of the donors were written (where they can still be seen) in gold letters above the bays which contained their books. As well as his books, Dr Gilbert also left, in 1743, £500 'for the purchase of busts of men eminent for learning to adorn the library'. With Gilbert's money, fourteen busts were commissioned from the Flemish sculptor Peter Scheemakers. These ranged in subject from Homer, Plato and Aristotle to Shakespeare, Newton, Robert Boyle and Archbishop Ussher (3). Other donors followed Gilbert's example, and by the mid-nineteenth century the Library possessed enough busts to fill all the spaces in the Long Room. The bust of Dean Swift by Roubilliac was commissioned by a class of Senior Sophisters (final year undergraduates) and is inscribed with the date 1745. The busts were originally placed level with the gallery, as can be seen in the Malton painting of the Long Room (8) but when

the ceiling level was altered in the nineteenth century they were brought down to their present position.

Most of the major changes which have subsequently taken place in the Old Library have been brought about by the need to provide additional accommodation for the Library's growing collection of books.

In 1800 the Library contained about 50,000 volumes. This number was then rapidly augmented in 1802 by the acquisition of the Fagel library, the biggest single collection ever received by the Library and one which increased the size of its collection by almost a half. Hendrik Baron Fagel had been Chief Minister of the Netherlands and when Napoleon invaded Holland he had fled to England with his books. The library was to have been sold at Christie's in March 1802, but the Erasmus Smith Board bought all 20,000 volumes and presented them to Trinity. It is not only the size of the collection which makes it

9. Eighteenth-century oak staircase in the Long Room.

10 (*opposite*). Plate from M. S. Merian's
Metamorphosis insectorum Surinamensium,
printed by J. Oosterwyk, Amsterdam, in 1719.
(Fagel collection.)

11 (*right*). Plate from *Das Römische Carneval*,
printed by J. F. Unger, Berlin, in 1789.
(Fagel collection.)

important but also the fact that it consists mainly of continental works – Dutch, French, German, Italian – which had been poorly represented in the Library hitherto **(10, 11)**. The Fagel collection was placed together in the large room at the east end of the Long Room (now at the top of the stairs leading from the Treasury) and special cases were constructed to hold the books.

Three years later, in 1805, the Library acquired another collection of great value, though tiny in size – the 127 volumes bequeathed by Henry George Quin. Quin, a Trinity graduate and book collector, bought at auction fine editions of Greek and Latin classical authors and Italian poets. Some of the books were already in superb bindings when he bought them; the others he had rebound by the great master-binders of his day **(12)**. In his will, Quin specified that the books should be preserved in his original bookcase, on which was to be inscribed 'Biblioteca Quiniana' in two-inch-high capital letters of gold. This was done and the bookcase stands in the east gallery of the Long Room.

The beginning of the nineteenth century heralded a change which fundamentally altered the status of the Library. In the seventeenth and eighteenth centuries the Library had acquired its books solely by purchase and through the generosity of bene-factors. Following the union of Great Britain and Ireland in 1801, the Copy-right Act extended to Trinity College the right to claim from every publisher in the British Isles one copy of each book, pamphlet, map and periodical which he

published, and this copy was to be deposited in the College Library. At first, the number of items received under the Copyright Act was not great, but increasing co-operation with the other copyright libraries, the Bodleian Library in Oxford, Cambridge Uni-versity Library, and the Faculty of

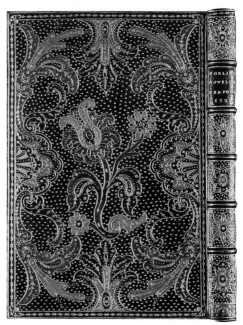

12. *Morlini nouellae* (Naples, 1520), from the Quin collection, showing the fine eighteenth-century binding, possibly by Derome of Paris.

13. *Book of Kells* – portrait of St Matthew (folio 28v).

14. *Book of Kells* – detail showing a human figure forming the initial H of Haec (folio 68v).

Advocates Library in Edinburgh (now the National Library of Scotland), has ensured that very little material of any scholarly value which is published in these islands is not now acquired by these libraries, where it is permanently preserved for the use of future generations. Even the political changes of the twentieth century have not altered the operation of this privilege, and successive British and Irish Copyright Acts have confirmed Trinity as a legal deposit library, receiving books from both countries. Some 60,000 volumes a year are now added to the collections, and these require over half a mile of additional shelving annually.

The acquisition of the Fagel collection in 1802 increased the size of the Library by almost a half at one fell swoop; the working of the Copyright Act brought about a sustained and ever more rapid growth in the bookstock. Gradually the bookcases in the Long Room filled up. The benches between them were removed and converted into low bookcases. Part of the gallery was ingeniously fitted with low mobile shelving, hinged to the wall and swinging out on curved tracks so that books could be stored on both sides. Some of this shelving is still in use.

By 1858 the Long Room was full and the College took the bold decision that major alterations to the building had to be made. They employed the architectural firm of Deane and Woodward, who advised that the flat eighteenth-century ceiling should be removed, and, if the level of the roof were raised, a new barrel-vaulted oak ceiling could be inserted, giving a great increase in the height of the room. This would then allow the gallery to be fitted with high bookcases, thereby producing a greater storage capacity in the room. Deane and Woodward's proposals were accepted and put into effect. Their alterations led to much public criticism at the time, but are now felt to have been a successful blending of the nineteenth century with the eighteenth **(front cover)**.

Less successful was the filling in of the Colonnades in 1891, another move designed to give the Library more accommodation for its growing number of books and readers but one which deprived the building of one of its major architectural features. Burgh's open arches underneath the Long Room were replaced by windows and two thirds of the ground floor space thus acquired was turned into a bookstack. The other third became a reading room.

Since this time, alterations to the structure of the Old Library have been relatively minor and have hardly affected its outward appearance or that of the Long Room. Before we pass on to the twentieth-century developments in the Library this seems an appropriate point to describe some of the items

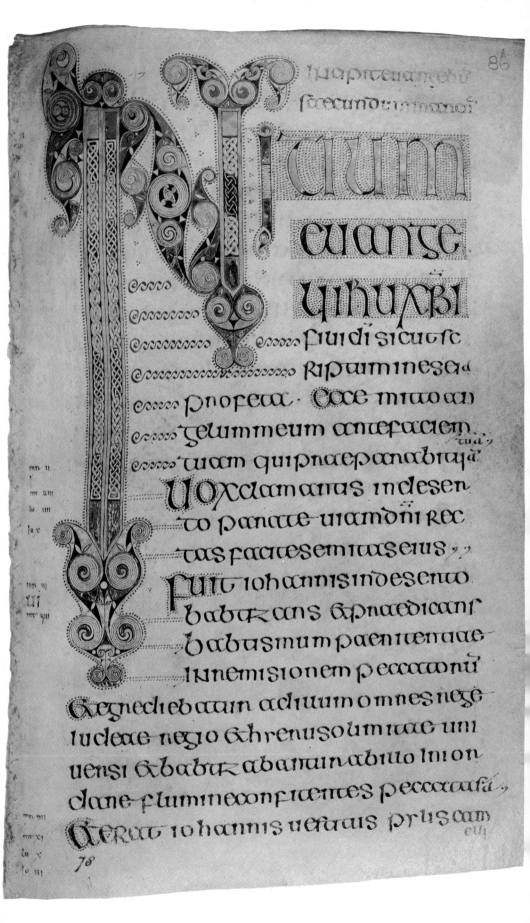

INapiteuangelii
secundummarcum

INItIuM
euange
IIhuxbi
fiIIdi sicutse
RIptuminesaia
pRofeta · ecce mittoan
geIummeum antefaciem
tuam quipraeparabituiã
uoxcIamantis indesen
to parate uiamdñi rec
tas facitesemitaseius
fuit iohannisindeserto
babtizans &praedicans
babtismum paenitentiae
inremisionem peccatorũ
&egrediebatur adillum omnesrege
iudeae regio &hierusolimitae uni
uersi &babtizabanturinabillo iniordane
flumineconfitentes peccatasua
&erat iohannis uestitus pilliscam

normally on display in the Old Library.

By far the most famous exhibit, and the one which all visitors come to see, is the *Book of Kells*. This magnificently illuminated manuscript was produced about the year AD 800 in a monastery scriptorium, but, as the manuscript displays artistic influences of Northumbria, Iona and Ireland, it is impossible to identify exactly where the monastery was situated. An account in the *Annals of Ulster* is believed to be the first record of the existence of the *Book*. The account describes its theft from Kells in 1007: 'the great Gospel of Colum Cille, the chief relic of the western world on account of its ornamented cover, was stolen by night from the western sacristy of the great stone church of Cenannus [Kells]. That Gospel was found after twenty nights and two months with its gold stolen from it, buried in the ground.' It presumably remained at Kells until the seventeenth century, when it was brought to Dublin for safe keeping during that troubled period and was presented to Trinity College by Henry Jones, Bishop of Meath.

The *Book* contains the Latin text of the four Gospels on 340 leaves of calf skin. It has a number of exquisite and intricate illuminations covering whole pages and almost every page of the text is accompanied by smaller painted decorations. There is a great emphasis on the symbols of the Evangelists – the man (Matthew), the lion (Mark), the calf (Luke) and the eagle (John). Three of the Gospels begin with a fully illustrated page showing these symbols together and they are constantly repeated in various forms **(flap)**. The *Book* also contains four 'portrait' pages, showing Christ, the Virgin and Child, St Matthew **(13)** and St John. Each Gospel begins its opening words with a richly ornamented page in which the text is submerged in the decoration, and

brightly coloured animals, faces and figures are often entwined into the capital letters at the beginning of lines of the ordinary text pages **(14)**. The *Book of Kells* was repaired and re-bound in four volumes in 1953.

The *Book of Durrow*, another donation by Bishop Jones of Meath, was written more than 100 years earlier than the *Book of Kells*. Its style is simpler but it too displays a highly developed sense of decoration as an accompaniment to the Gospels in Latin. The text of each Gospel begins with an elaborate capital letter occupying a large part of the page **(15)** and facing this is a so-called 'carpet page' – a full page of intricate, abstract designs. The *Book of Durrow* was originally kept in a silver-plated wooden shrine, which is unfortunately now lost.

The *Book of Armagh* is the only known example where the whole Latin text of the New Testament has survived in the form in which it was used in the Celtic Church. The *Book* also contains the lives of St Patrick and St Martin, as well as the Confession of St Patrick. From evidence in the manuscript itself, it can be dated to around AD 807. As with other manuscripts in the Insular tradition, the symbols of the four Evangelists appear together on the same page, but here they are much starker and less decorated than, for example, in the *Book of Kells* **(16)**.

The *Book of Dimma*, another Gospel book, contains in addition some sections of liturgical text. The name 'Dimma' comes from an inscription which appears in the manuscript at the end of St John's Gospel: 'Finit amen – Dimma Macc Nathi'. The *Book* has a silver shrine dating from about 1150 **(17)**. Such book shrines, which are peculiar to Ireland and Scotland, were used to house and protect the book, which had acquired an importance of its own as a holy relic. Most shrines, as in the case of *Durrow*, have been lost, and so the Shrine of *Dimma* is particularly significant.

15. *Book of Durrow* – the 'initium'. Mark 1, 1 (folio 86r).

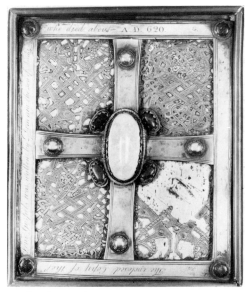

17. The shrine of the *Book of Dimma* (about 1150).

As well as the manuscripts, the Old Library exhibits an elaborately carved Irish harp, given to the College by William Conyngham in the eighteenth century **(18)**. Legend has it that the harp belonged to Brian Boru, who died at the Battle of Clontarf in 1014, but evidence for this is lacking. All that one can say for certain is that it is at least 500 years old and is the finest known example of this traditional Irish instrument.

Let us now return to the beginning of the twentieth century and the Library's constant shortage of space. By this time the Copyright Act was being enforced more effectively, with the result that by the 1920s the shelves were again full and books were being stored in piles in the Long Room. The College decided that, as no further space could be created in the Old Library, the solution was to build a completely new reading room and to convert the reading room in the Colonnades into storage space for books, thus making the whole of this area a bookstack.

A Hall of Honour, which was to be built in memory of those members of the College who had fallen in the First World War, would serve as an entrance to the new reading room. The Hall of

16 (*opposite*). *Book of Armagh* – the symbols of the four Evangelists (folio 32v).

Honour was opened in 1928 and the Reading Room in 1937. The room, now known as the 1937 Reading Room, is an octagonal building, inspired by the great circular reading room of the British Museum **(19)**. It provided more than twice as many seats for readers as had been available in the old reading room and contained, in addition, underground stack space. Books requested by readers were transported from the Old Library to the Reading Room by means of a conveyor belt below the pathway separating the two buildings.

Thomas Burgh and the eighteenth-century Fellows of the College had built a library which, in one building, had provided space for books and readers for 200 years. With the opening of the 1937 Reading Room began the

18. Irish harp.

homo   leo

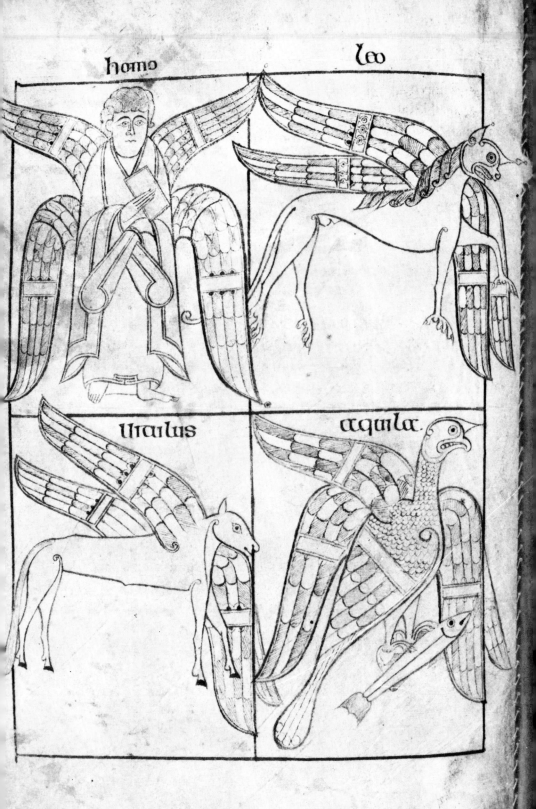

uitulus   aquila

19. The 1937 Reading Room.

20. The Berkeley Library.

unfortunate process of providing for the Library's growing needs by adding to the number of buildings which it occupied. The financial constraints of the twentieth century have also meant that, instead of producing adequate space for another 200 years, each new library building has been full within a matter of decades of its completion.

By the 1950s the Library was again looking for space, and an appeal was launched to secure funds for another new library building. Support came from many sources, including graduates of the College, private benefactors and the Irish Government, and in 1960 an international architectural competition was held. From over 200 entries, an English architect, Paul Koralek, was selected as the winner. His library, since named the Berkeley Library, after the philosopher and former Librarian George Berkeley, was opened in 1967 by Eamon De Valera, the President of Ireland **(20)**.

21. The Berkeley Library.

The architect was required to produce a building which would act as the hub of the growing Library complex and would, at the same time, be a fitting complement to the existing College buildings. Situated between the sober, classical, Old Library and the highly ornamented, Italianate, Museum Building, Koralek's library is a building stark in its modernity. It is constructed of granite and reinforced concrete, which is exposed both inside and out, leaving visible the marks of the shuttering used in its construction **(21)**. The building contains space for nearly a million volumes, most of which are housed on two floors of subterranean stack area. The upper floors contain open-access bookstacks and reader places arranged in a way which allows the reader a certain amount of seclusion and at the same time easy access to the most important books on his subject. On the ground floor is the main reference area, the enquiry desk and the Library's catalogues, together with administrative and processing departments. From this building is also operated the Library's Information Service, which provides information and documentation for government departments, research bodies and commercial organisations.

At the same time that the Berkeley Library was built, the east end of the Old Library was remodelled, also by Koralek, to provide a reading room for the older and more valuable books. To mark the College's quatercentenary in 1992, part of the Colonnades was converted into a new gallery for changing exhibitions. A new Treasury was built for the Book of Kells and the highly successful Library Shop was enlarged.

The collection of manuscripts, as well as that of printed books, has continued to grow over the centuries, adding not only further medieval manuscripts like the *Book of Armagh* **(16)** and the *Book of Dimma* **(17)** and important manuscripts in the Irish language, but also more modern papers, such as the autobiography of Dean Swift **(22, 23)**, George Berkeley's introduction to the

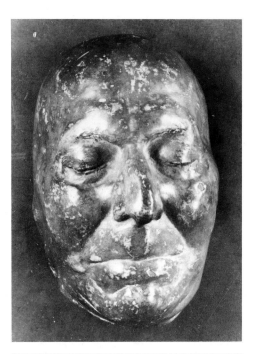

Principles of Human Knowledge and, more recently, the papers of the two Irish dramatists J. M. Synge **(24, 25)** and Samuel Beckett **(26)**.

In the 1970s work was carried out on the West Pavilion of the Old Library to provide a greatly enlarged Manuscripts Department and an air-conditioned strong room for the manuscripts. The third floor was at the same time converted into a Conservation Laboratory. This excellently equipped and purpose-built conservation studio is responsible for the repair and preservation of the Library's books and manuscripts. All types of conservation work are undertaken. Examples of its work on manuscripts are the elaborate restoration of the *Book of Mulling*, an eighth-century Irish Gospel book on vellum **(27)**, and the repair of a collection of seventeenth-century letters which were suffering from both mould damage and the effect which the acid in the ink had had on the paper over three centuries. The letters have been de-acidified and the holes in the paper filled in with special tissue **(28)**. Another recent project involved the complete dismemberment of an early sixteenth-century printed book, the washing and de-acidification of each individual page and then the re-sewing and rebinding of the repaired volume, preserving all the original boards and binding components **(29)**. The Conservation Laboratory combines the traditional craftsmanship of the bookbinder and print repairer with the new skills and modern scientific techniques of paper and parchment repair and conservation.

As the books and periodicals continued to flow into the Library, it became obvious that Koralek's new building would not contain enough space to store them and that, instead of

22 (*above left*). Swift's death mask.

23 (*left*). Dean Swift's autobiography, in which, as a student at Trinity, he writes of his lack of interest in studying.

changes have been made taken place, that it was not worth while to

deal with in the text.

In ~~what~~ follows I have given a direct account of my life on

the islands, and what I met with among them, inventing nothing, and

changing nothing ~~in its essence~~. As far as possible, however, I have

disguised the indentity of the people I speak of, by making

changes in thier names, ~~the places of their homes~~, in the letters

~~that~~ I quote, and ~~in their~~ family relationships. I have had nothing

to say about them that was not wholly in their favour, but I have

made this disguise to keep them from ever feeling that a too

direct use had been made of thier kindness, and friendship for

which I am more grateful than it is easy to say.

24. Page of the typescript of J. M. Synge's *Aran Islands.*

25. Synge's typewriter.

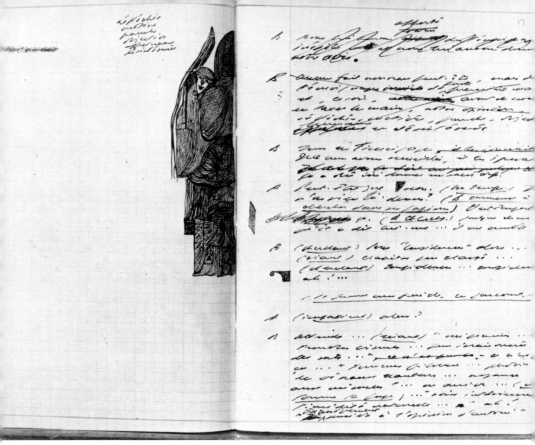

using valuable space on the College campus for another huge bookstack, it would be more effective to store the less heavily-used volumes away from the College. A book repository was built near Dublin Airport and this is operated and occupied jointly by Trinity College Library, the National Library of Ireland and Dublin Public Libraries.

With the opening of the Arts and Social Sciences Building in 1978 the College acquired a new square, Fellows' Square (30). It is bounded on each side by a library building. To the north is the Old Library, to the west the 1937 Reading Room, to the east Koralek's Berkeley Library and to the south, completing the square, the Arts Building, also by Koralek, of which two of the floors are largely given over to library space. This Library, named the Lecky Library after the well-known historian who was a graduate of the College, houses the main collections for the social sciences and modern languages. Much of the starkness of Koralek's earlier Berkeley Library has

26. Page from a manuscript of Samuel Beckett, showing a fragment of an abandoned play in French and the author's doodles.

27. *Book of Mulling* – portrait of St John (folio 80). The book was repaired in the Library's Conservation Laboratory.

28. Conservation Laboratory – repairing damaged manuscripts.

29. Conservation Laboratory – repair work on *The worlde and the chylde* (1522).

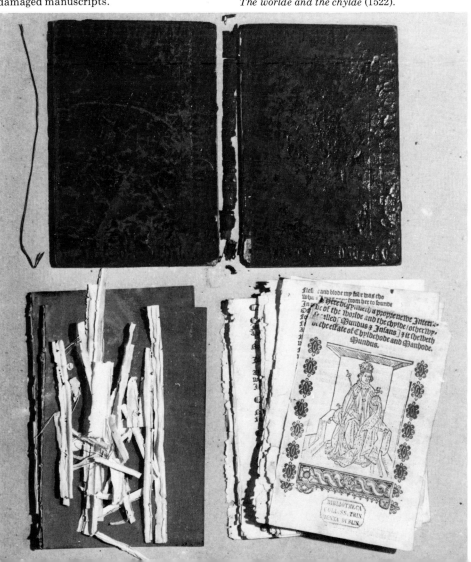

30. Fellows' Square, showing, in the left foreground the 1937 Reading Room, behind it the Old Library, to the right the Berkeley Library and in the right foreground the Arts Building, which contains the Lecky Library.

31. The Lecky Library.

been softened; the concrete walls are smooth and do not display the marks of the shuttering; the floor is covered with carpet; the enquiry counters are of pine, not reinforced concrete. It is a warmer, more friendly library to work in and is particularly popular with students (31).

A similarly comfortable well-equipped library for students in the sciences was opened in 1992, in the William Rowan Hamilton Building, at the centre of the science buildings at the east end of the College.

As we look towards the beginning of the twenty-first century, more and more information is becoming available in electronic form. But whatever developments the new technology brings about in libraries, there will always be a need for major libraries like that of Trinity College Dublin to continue to collect, store and preserve the book, the manuscript, the map and the periodical in order to make the scholarship of yesterday and today available to the scholar of tomorrow.

Title page of *Thystorye of the right noble and worthy knyght Parys and of the fayre Vyenne the dolphyns daughter of Vyennoys*, translated from the French by William Caxton. Trinity's is the only known copy of this book, printed by Gerard Leeu in Antwerp in 1492.

Title page of *The worlde and the chylde*, printed by Wynkyn de Worde in London in 1522. Trinity's is the only known copy of the fifth English play to be issued in print.

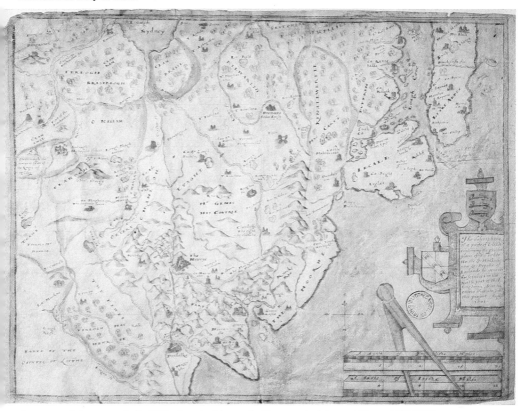

A manuscript map made in 1602 of part of Armagh, Tyrone, Antrim and Down (MS 2379).

Title page of A. Munting's *Nauwkeurige beschryving der aardgewassen*
(Leyden 1696), showing gold-leaf letterpress ornamentation. (Fagel collection.)